DON'T HURRY ME – I'M SUFFOLK

Celebrating the 'Curious County'

Charlie Haylock

with illustrations by Barrie Appleby

COUNTRYSIDE BOOKS

NEWBURY, BERKSHIRE

First published 2013
© Charlie Haylock 2013

COUNTRYSIDE BOOKS
3 Catherine Road
Newbury, Berkshire

To view our complete range of books,
please visit us at
www.countrysidebooks.co.uk

ISBN 978 1 84674 314 6

**Supporting St Edmund
for England**

Designed by Peter Davies, Nautilus Design
Front cover photograph by Sylvia Bickers

Produced through The Letterworks Ltd., Reading
Typeset by CJWT Solutions, St Helens
Printed by Berforts Information Press, Oxford

CONTENTS

ACKNOWLEDGEMENTS

I would like to thank the following people, organisations, societies, associations and companies for helping me in my research. Without their input this book would never have been written. I apologise for any one I might have mistakenly missed out. But I thank you too.

Once again a special thank you to BBC Radio Suffolk, and in particular, Lesley Dolphin and all the listeners.

W. Alecock McMahon
Barrie Appleby
Jason Appleby
Ark Design Consultancy
Aspall Cyder
John Barnes
David Bartholomew
BBC Radio Suffolk & Listeners
Sylvia Bickers
Sue Brotherwood
Barry Chevallier Guild
Lesley Dolphin
Darren Dourdoy
Gavin Downes
East Anglian Daily Times
Edwardstone White Horse PH
Eel's Foot PH
Gale
Rex Garrod
Sally Garrod
Greene King PLC
Lisa Harris
Bill Haylock
Jenny Hursell
Peter Jones
Julie Jordan & Jerv's Mate Fred
Long Shop Museum
Anna Mercer
Middleton Bell PH
Keith Morling

Miss Maureen Mothersole
Nick & Trish Musgrove
Mark Murphy
Museum of East Anglian Life
John Mutimer
Mary Oliver
Old Glory Molly (the original)
Alan Riddleston
Chris Ridgeon
Darren Rozier
Wendy Sadler
St Edmundsbury Borough Council,
    Heritage Service
St. Mary's Church, Erwarton
Paul Scriven
Charlotte Smith
Clorinda Smith
Paul Stockdale
Southwold Museum
Sudbury Town Council
Suffolk Punch Trust
Suffolk Record Office Bury St Edmunds
    Ipswich & Lowestoft
The Jerv Jordan Collection
The Windmill House Collection
Keith Walladge
Dave & Kath Whiting
Vonny & Eileen Whymark
Gary Wilson
Patricia Winfield

Thank yer koindly t'gether!

INTRODUCTION

Over the years I have compiled quite a bank of an eclectic array of Suffolk curios, that sometimes just fill me full of wonder, amazement and some in total disbelief. *Howsumever*, some are horrid and awful, but still go together to make an intriguing history of Suffolk.

I have picked up these curious gems from a number of sources. . . from my family, especially my grandad Bill Haylock, the story teller, who was very proud of being Suffolk. . . . from the research I've done compiling five books about Suffolk. . . from all the lovely people that come up after my talks, to give me snippets of Suffolk oddities and rarities. . . from the owd Suffolkers who see me after my eccentric one man show and want to pass on little Suffolk anecdotes. . . from appearing regularly on *BBC Radio Suffolk* with my weekly, 'Haylock's Half Hour for Forty Minutes', and getting wonderful responses from the listeners. . . and from listening. . . to the many knowledgeable Suffolk people who are proud of their unique historic county, who want to share their knowledge, for other people to know. . . and benefit.

Recently I have gained even more interesting facts about Suffolk, from the reading and studying I have to do with my latest venture. This is with the internationally famed cartoonist, Barrie Appleby. . . a weekly Saturday cartoon on Suffolk current affairs called 'Charlie's News Quips', that appears in the East Anglian Daily Times.

As Suffolk has been rebranded the 'Curious County' by 'Visit Suffolk', I thought it a good opportunity to have a curious look at this ancient county . . . who is the Royal Farter? . . . who was the naked Suffolk dancer who performed before the King? . . . Is Lord Nelson really half Suffolk?. . . Does Sir Donald Bradman really have Suffolk roots? This book will have the answers. . . and more. . . much much more!

I'm privileged yet again to have Barrie Appleby illustrating some of these wonderful oddities. I hope you enjoy reading 'Don't Hurry Me – I'm Suffolk', as much as I did compiling it.

Charlie Haylock

5

CHAPTER 1

An Eccentric Suffolk Inventor

Suffolk can boast that a very lovely man from Mickfield, Doctor Rex Garrod, is truly an eccentric inventor in the true mould of film and fiction. He's an absolute 'must' in a book about curious Suffolk. It has been said, that if he had lived in medieval times, he would have worn a tall pointed hat and had a long white beard. And in today's times he would have been quite at ease playing the part of Q in the James Bond films … in real life! He could also be called a 'Time Lord' as you will see later.

Rex is still living in the house he built, in the village of Mickfield where he was born and bred. But don't let this fool you. Rex has brought pleasure to millions, has been an inspirational educationalist, and helped countless disabled people to do things they thought they could only dream about.

Rex's irrepressible enthusiasm and anarchic good humour brings things alive, and has helped thousands of young people to learn, by doing things and making things, and having great fun in the process. We can only speculate how many careers and life long interests have been started and influenced by the Mickfield Merlin.

Rex's daughter testing out props for Mercury Theatre's 'Wizard of Oz'

Rex had humble beginnings going to the local school. He then became an apprentice electrician and a semi-professional speedway rider with Ipswich Witches and Scunthorpe. Later he was the sidecar passenger for Dave Bickers, the famous motocross world champion. This last fact alone will tell you what sort of man Rex is. Some say it takes someone with a special skill to ride passenger in a motorbike and sidecar race. This may be the case, but you've also got to be some kind of a nut. Rex fits the bill perfectly. I'm not talking out of tune here, because the notice on Rex's workshop door as you go in, reads quite simply -

REX GARROD
SPECIAL EFFECTS
Workshop

WARNING!

MAY CONTAIN A NUT !

It was his apprenticeship with Bill Bunn, a local Suffolk self employed electrician, that sparked Rex's curiosity in how things worked. Bill told Rex that you can't repair anything in practice unless you know how it works in theory. This excellent but simple concept, combined with Rex's natural artistic ability, ensured a career in animatronics, model making and special effects for TV, films and museums.

Rex's initiation into the film industry was to make all the weapons for the film '*Krull*'. He then went to work with Dave Bickers on various films including '*Pink Panther*' and '*An American Werewolf in London*'. Gradually Rex's career widened to include model making and visual effects and he worked on the Anglia TV series, '*Tales of the Unexpected*'.

A number of joint ventures with Tim Hunkin, another inventor, followed. These included the successful TV series, 'The Secret Life of Machines', in which Rex and Tim co-presented. They explored the workings of machines and domestic appliances, and used them to creatively explain scientific and mechanical principles.

Rex sitting on a pile of washing machines

Rex made 'Roland Rat's' car that led to a long and successful relationship with 'Ragdoll Productions' making fascinating models for, 'Rosie and Jim', 'Tots TV' and 'Teletubbies'. It was during Rex's time with 'Ragdoll' that he made BRUM, the little radio controlled car that went on many an adventure enthralling young and excited TV viewers everywhere. BRUM was a highly sophisticated piece of engineering equipment, using twenty two radio control channels and two operators. An example of innocent and playful imagery, achieved by using the most advanced technology and Rex's design skills.

Rex and BRUM

Rex has designed and made special devices and control systems for a number of people with serious disabilities. The most outstanding creation Rex ever made, and the one he is most proud of, was helping Trevor Jones, a helicopter pilot, to fly again.

Trevor had once bravely saved the life of Richard Branson in one of Richard's ballooning escapades. It was a daring aerial manoeuvre, and fair to say, that Richard Branson is alive and well today thanks to the bravery of Trevor Jones.   He was a very skilled and accomplished pilot, but unfortunately, whilst on a skiing holiday soon afterwards, had an horrendous accident that left him completely paralysed - except for the use of one thumb and some head movement. That is all!

Rex converted a Microlite Shadow aircraft, and this enabled Trevor to fly solo again, using just one thumb and head movement. Rex designed and made the complex control systems, intricately and accurately made to measure for Trevor. The Civil Aviation Authority completed all their stringent tests and investigations. Everything was in order and all safety checks were passed. *And soon very after*, Trevor Jones completed a solo flight over the English Channel.

Rex has always worked closely with young engineers, promoting science and engineering in schools and colleges around the country. He is a tireless supporter of design and technology among our young people. He has made hundreds of visits and given countless lectures in schools, young engineer clubs, and science fairs across the UK, sharing his considerable knowledge of how things work, and the scientific principles behind them.

When he took part in BBC2's series 'Robot Wars', Rex was the key figure. He created robots 'Recyclopse', 'Robot the Bruce' and 'Cassius', who were the stars of the first and second series. 'Robot Wars' was to lead to national and international interest in engineering for young people. When the 'Young Engineers' asked him to run a 'Rex's Robot Challenge', he was absolutely thrilled and delighted. Rex was over the moon with their enthusiasm, and was assured in knowing that some of his skill, knowledge and inspiration was being passed on to future generations.

Rex and a warring robot

When explaining how he built the robots, Rex comments on the fact that he originally had two aerials on the robot, but this didn't work. Because they fell in love with one another and got married ... The wedding was awful, but the reception was brilliant!

Another example of Rex's eccentricity, was when he was in a motorway café on his way back from a studio somewhere. He was recognised by a couple of schoolboys who came up and asked if they could ask him a few questions. The schoolboys were part of a school trip and their mini-bus was in the car park. The boys were told that once Rex had finished his meal, he would have a word with their master.

Unbeknown to everyone, Rex had a couple of his robots in his van, and it wasn't long afore there was a large area of the car park sectioned off and some very happy kids having a go at the controls of the robots as they whizzed round the car park ... even the master as well ... something they all will remember and treasure for always.

Rex also has a passion for clocks, and has been involved in several projects in producing some wonderful eccentric clocks for public display ... made out of dustbin lids, old parts of this, that and the other, recycled bits of old fandangled thingamebobs and unusable bits that other people would throw away. They are truly magnificent inventions in the Chittychittybangbang mould. Examples of these wonderful time pieces can be seen at Watermouth Castle near Ilfracombe in the West Country, and here at Charlie Mannings Amusement Park in Felixstowe. Along with Tim Hunkin and Andy Plant, Rex has helped create a number of these wonderful tick tocking oddities. They bring pleasure to the thousands that pass by, and put lots of smiles on people's faces ... that's what true eccentrics do. And believe it or not, they keep pretty good time to say the least...and not just for show. Rex is definitely a 'Time Lord'.

Pencil sketch – Rex and car and robot and clock, by Brian Knight

Rex has been called several names – inventor ... Mr Fix It ... and many more. But Rex likes to refer to *hisself* as a Professional Bodgineer! He hasn't got a single academic qualification, but in October 2005 the Degree of Doctor of Civil Law *honoris causa* was conferred upon him by the University of East Anglia ... richly deserved.

I give you three extracts from the *'Oration for Rex Garrod'*, at this auspicious occasion in October 2005, including the last paragraph.

'... he has, in his own life,
learned through the love of his subject,
following his own curiosity,
using his huge energy and ability
to become an international figure in his field.'

'... whether you want to know about the history of science,
the principles of physics,
the workings of anything mechanical,
or even the best remedy for gunpowder,
... Rex is your man'

'... And so we come to why Rex is here today.
He is a man whose determination, enthusiasm, skill and knowledge,
have excited us, entertained us and educated us. He has worked on a
worldwide stage and in our own community,
and for some people
he has quite literally made possible
what seemed impossible.

Pro-Vice Chairman, Ladies and Gentlemen ...

Rex Garrod'

Rex is rather pleased and proud that he is now a Doctor, but his anarchic good humour still shows through … and I quote him once more,

'… one of the benefits of being a Doctor
… is that it will be easier for me,
to get the dangerous chemicals I use!'

All photographs in this section have been supplied courtesy of Rex and Sally Garrod.

CHAPTER 2

Dastardly Suffolk!

Suffolk have had some famous, dastardly characters in the past, some of whom have been held up to be virtuous characters … but underneath … are selfish and wicked. Others are just plain evil, as you'll see from my account of the most celebrated murder in Suffolk. But having said that, the wicked and blood thirsty way the murderer was dealt with … with thousands turning up to watch and bay … makes today's times look harmless, demure and genteel. Suffolk was indeed a harsh place to live.

Simon de Sudbury (Simon Theobald)

Simon Theobald, (and there are still people with that surname living in the area), was born in 1318 to a prominent wealthy Sudbury family in the cloth trade. He was a bright and clever lad and eventually entered university in Paris. He could wheel and deal, and cunningly knew which moves to make. Very quickly he was noticed and became chaplain to Pope Innocent VI. In 1361 Simon was installed as Bishop of London and very soon became ambassador to King Edward III.

After a few years, in 1375, he was enthroned as the Archbishop of Canterbury, and in 1380 became the Lord Chancellor. Simon had cunningly engineered his way around. Skulduggery was the by word and the principle he worked to. He was now the most powerful man in the Kingdom, other than the King, who by this time was Richard II.

Simon obviously . . . was not so Silly Suffolk! But that was all about to change!

Oh Yes!

Simon's brief life at the top of the pile literally went to his head, and would come to a very abrupt and gory end. He had the unwise notion of inflicting a poll tax on the people of England (nothing changes!). This was to help raise money to finance a war against France. The tax was levied on all those over the age of fifteen, at the exorbitant flat rate of three groats per person … large families were particularly hit the hardest.

(A groat was four pence. Which meant the people were being taxed one whole shilling. Which in today's money would be extortionate, as it was then.)

The peasants were revolting (especially those from north of the Waveney!), and were led by one Wat Tyler, who was also a Suffolk man (this fact has recently been established by historians with hard evidence showing that he was born and bred in Hadleigh, Suffolk).

In 1381 the mob attacked Lambeth Palace and Simon fled to the Tower of London for protection. But so unpopular was he, that the guards just let the revolting peasants pass through unchallenged, (should never have brought in a poll tax!). He was then taken unceremoniously to Tower Hill, where he was brutally hacked to death, and his severed head was impaled and put on display on a spike at London Bridge. His tortured body was buried at Canterbury Cathedral, but his head was brought back to Sudbury, to be kept in St Gregory's Church. The skull is still there to this day! It's housed in a special niche in the vestry. (Wonderful sight).

Simon's Skull
(Courtesy of St Edmundsbury Borough Council, Heritage Service)

In fact, to hide his dastardly scheming, Simon actually carried out lots of good deeds, which included founding a college for priests-in-waiting in his home town of Sudbury, on the site of the present day Walnuttree Hospital. His good side was recognised by the town, and the Sudbury coat of arms has included in it the talbot dog, which was prominent in Simon's badge and his own coat of arms.

Suffolk Sudbury coat of arms
(Courtesy of Sue Brotherwood, Sudbury Town Council)

This part of Suffolk was now firmly on the map, especially when its famous local lad went by the name of Simon de Sudbury who had become both Archbishop of Canterbury and Lord Chancellor. Most probably he would have become a well respected historical figure, and known for his good deeds … but what did the *duzzy bugger* go and do? He brought in a poll tax and lost his 'street cred', along with his head !

Thomas Wolsey (later Cardinal Wolsey)

This famous *Ipsidge* boy was also going to become the most powerful man in England, second only to Henry VIII. But pride came before a fall, and he died on his way to be tried for treason. This was punishable by death, and the verdict was usually a foregone conclusion. His untimely demise meant he escaped being beheaded ... what lengths some people go to ... just to avoid the issue.

Thomas Wolsey (but pronounced 'Wulcy' by the man *hisself* ... I would never admit to a name like that in such a macho world at the time ... *caw'd a hell* no!), was born about 1474, to a wealthy family in *Ipsidge*. The folklore of him being a poor butcher's son, and going from rags to riches is sheer myth and an embellishment of the true story (sorry about that).

(Courtesy of Edwardstone White Horse)

He had an exceptional mind, which is a polite way of saying he could outwit and fool all that came within his circle, and at the young age of only fifteen, he was granted a degree at Oxford University. He gained the nickname, 'Boy Bachelor', and by 1497 was awarded a full fellowship at Magdalen College (pronounced *Mawdlen* College, which is the Angle pronunciation as opposed to the Saxon one).

In 1498 Thomas was ordained as a priest, and thereafter gained many ecclesiastical posts, which he held all at the same time. He was noted for his administrative skills, and streamlining bureaucracy (which means he was a selfish, ruthless and dastardly man), and started to become a favourite of King Henry VII. This favouritism continued during the reign of King Henry VIII, and administrative posts were now being piled on to his long list of positions. Eventually in 1551 he became Archbishop of York, Cardinal 'Wulcy', and Lord Chancellor....he was now the most powerful man in all England, whose wealth equalled that of the Crown ... and he still wanted more ... he had two failed attempts to become Pope ... Mind you ... if he had achieved this exalted position, he certainly would not have been able to take on the names of 'Pious' or 'Innocent' ... not with his life style (especially when he had a live-in mistress, Joan Larke, and two illegitimate children).

His lavishness and extravagance was making 'Wulcy' a very unpopular person throughout the land, and indeed, abroad. He had an obsession for building grand palaces, colleges and the like. These included Hampton Court, York Palace, Cardinal College at Oxford (renamed twice since, and now Christ College), and of course Wolsey College in Ipswich, of which Wolsey's Gate is the only thing left standing.

'Oi've bin knock'n on 'iss door fer thutty minnuts ... 'n' no bugger's answer'd!'

(Courtesy of Suffolk Record Office – Ipswich – ref K681/1/262/484)

To accommodate his excessive and greedy life style, and to finance some of Henry VIII's schemes and projects, Wolsey had imposed many crippling taxes ... here we go again! When will they ever learn? ... This added to the growing hatred of him amongst the population, and in particular, by many of the influential group which surrounded the King ... not a good move! He had been taken over by greed.

Then the proverbial hit the fan! Henry VIII asked Wolsey for help in obtaining a divorce from Catherine of Aragon. This was to prove costly for Wolsey. He came up against Papal opposition, and also the wrath of the powerful Boleyn family, who were favoured by the King, especially as Anne was the next intended. The snail's pace at which all the wheeling and dealing was taking place, was now annoying both Anne and Henry immensely. This was not a very sensible thing to do!

He was forced to resign as Lord Chancellor, and give up the Great Seal of England. He lost all but one of his high ranking positions, and all his possessions were assigned over to the King.

Wolsey was now on a downward spiral, and there appeared to be no escape.

He continued his role as the Archbishop of York, and his only place of residence now was in York, and most humble, compared with his previous life style. But by 1530, Henry had lost all patience, and accused Wolsey of treason. He was arrested whilst having a meal and told to immediately pack and head for London to stand trial. It was odds on that he would be found guilty and with it, the death penalty. *Howsumever*, on his way from York to London, he was taken ill and died on an overnight stop in Leicester Abbey, where he was laid to rest – (and not under a car park alongside Richard III neither).

So Thomas did elude the axeman after all.

William Corder and the Murder of Maria Marten

How could I not mention, 'The Red Barn Murder', and the two principal characters? William Corder and Maria Marten, (christened Martin, only to be changed after her death. London reporters misspelt the name on hearing the Suffolk pronunciation of her surname).

In the official account of the events leading up to, and including the trial of William Corder for Maria's murder, it is written that:-

Drawing of Maria Marten
(Courtesy of Suffolk Record Office – Ipswich,
ref – Trial of William Corder 345.02523)

'I never knew or heard of a case in my life which abounded with so many extraordinary incidents as the present. It really appears more like a

romance than a tale of common life; and were it not that the circumstances were so well authenticated, it would appear absolutely incredible; it, however, verifies the remark of Lord Byron, that 'truth is stranger than fiction'.

Maria was born in Polstead, Suffolk, in 1801, the daughter of a farm labourer and mole catcher. Her mother sadly died when Maria was only ten years old. This immediately dispels the folk lore and fables, that it was Maria's mother who had the famous dreams about her daughter's death. A year later, her father remarried Anne Golden, much younger than *hisself*, and only a few years older than Maria.

As a teenager, Maria appears to have been a very 'sociable' girl, and 'put herself about' somewhat. She certainly did catch the eye of many a young man. Her first affair was with Thomas Corder, a farmer's son, and resulted in a daughter, Matilda, who only lived for three weeks or so. After the burial in Polstead Church, Thomas ended the affair.

Maria's second affair was with Peter Matthews, who was associated with Polstead Hall in some way. Again, Maria fell pregnant, and gave birth to Thomas in 1824. Matthews regularly sent maintenance, and as usual in these cases, 'dumped' her with no thoughts of marriage at all. Maria looked after young Thomas at her family home with her father and stepmother.

Her third affair, which proved to be a fatal attraction, was with the dastardly William Corder, brother of the previous Thomas Corder ... you can now see why I called her a very 'sociable' girl. And yes! You've guessed it ... Maria became pregnant again.

'Arrangements' were made to have the baby away from Polstead. This she did, but upon her return, the baby died only some weeks old. The baby was buried, but not in the churchyard. Maria's father tried to bring pressure to bear on William to marry his daughter. Corder agreed to take Maria to *Ipsidge* and do the decent thing. In the meantime, the local constable, John Baalham (whose direct descendants still live in the area today), was given a warrant to be served on Maria, for the, **'Apprehension to giving birth to illegitimate children'** ... (he'd have had more than his fair share of work in this day and age!) ... but, he never issued the warrant. It's believed he didn't have the heart to arrest Maria ... but in a curious sort of way, if he had've done, he most probably would have saved her from being murdered ... we will never know.

Corder agreed to meet Maria in the Red Barn around about lunchtime on that fateful day in May. Maria was to dress as a man, so in her disguise, no-one would see her leaving. They met in the barn, and William Corder, who like all the others, had no intention of marriage … she could pick 'em … *caw'd a hell* yes! Maria was murdered, and her body was put into a shallow grave in the barn.

William concocted stories about Maria's whereabouts saying they'd moved to London. But his intentions were to start a new life … he even advertised for a wife in the newspapers. He quickly found a partner, married and made plans for the future.

The plot thickens … Meanwhile, back at base, Maria's stepmother had three dreams saying her stepdaughter had been murdered, and lay under the floor of the Red Barn. Each dream was more specific than the previous. The father decided to investigate, and found his daughter's body, lying in a shallow grave, exactly where his wife had said. It was rumoured that the stepmother was somehow involved, and also had an affair with William Corder … (makes the plots in the TV soaps somewhat tame).

After some searching, Corder was arrested in London, brought back to Polstead and the inquest took place in the Cock Inn (at a later date the Cock Inn became Cock Farm, and the present day Cock Inn, on the village green, is not where the inquest took place). He then went to Bury St Edmunds for trial, and was duly found guilty after a two day court hearing … (how long would that take today?) He was to be hanged in public on Monday 11th August 1828. Roughly twenty thousand people turned up to watch this public spectacle … from all over East Anglia and further afield. Over two hundred went from the little village of Boxford alone … Bloodthirsty Lot !

The gruesome tale still unfolds. After the hanging, the hangman received a *tidily sum* from the highest bidder for the hang rope. This unofficial auction was the scene of much jostling and shouting (similar to the January sales at Harrods … nigh on a riot). Worse to come! . . At Shire Hall, the surgeons cut and folded back the skin to expose Corder's chest muscles for public display … many thousands filed passed this grisly sight (think I'd rather watch a TV soap after all … and that's saying *suffen*!) Next day, at the County Hospital, in front of an audience of medical students and the like, Corder was skinned, and then his body dissected bit by bit for medical research. The skin was not thrown away … Oh no! … it was tanned to become more leathery, and the official account of the trial was

Corder awaiting execution. (Courtesy of Suffolk Record Office – Bury St Edmunds ref – Maria Marten by J. Curtis 1948)

(Courtesy of Suffolk Record Office – Bury St Edmunds ref – Maria Marten by J. Curtis 1948)

bound with Corder's own skin, and can be seen today in Moyes's Hall Museum, Bury St Edmunds, alongside the death mask.

And there's more! His skeleton was reassembled and used for medical teaching in the West Suffolk Hospital, later to be removed to the Hunterian Museum in the Royal College of Surgeons till 2004. It was only then, that descendants of William Corder, were able to cremate their evil predecessor and finally put this gruesome tale to rest.

The Red Barn Murder has become the subject of many plays, stories, and even film, which has made it into, most probably, Suffolk's most famous and notable murder.

Many books have been *writ* on the subject of The Red Barn, but my favourite must be the one *writ* by J. Curtis in 1941, with the very long title of :-

DON'T HURRY ME – I'M SUFFOLK

'An authentic and faithful history
of the mysterious murder
of Maria Marten
and a full development
of the extraordinary circumstances
which led to the discovery of her body
in the Red Barn
to which is added
the trial of William Corder'

Can you imagine asking for that title in the book shop?

CHAPTER 3

Suffolk Curiosities

Recently, Suffolk has been rebranded as '**The Curious County**' by *Visit Suffolk*. This is an attempt to try and promote tourism and seduce *furreners* to admire Suffolk's wonderful heritage coastline, to relax amidst the countless beauty spots in the countryside, to mingle in our historic towns and villages, and to marvel at our ancient buildings and museums.

Therefore it's only apt for me to record some of the Curious County's curious facts.

This is an historical account of Suffolk's oddities and not so well known snippets. To perhaps destroy some Suffolk myths and legends and to confirm a few others. To hopefully come up with some previously unknowns that makes Suffolk so wonderfully unique.

I have categorised this pot pourri in some sort of chronological order, with a semblance of sensibility. But when that's not possible, then I've resorted to alphabetical. If you're Suffolk, you'll easily follow the drift and line of thought. *Howsumever*, if you're a *furrener* … then please … *do you* enjoy the learning curve.

(*Courtesy of* East Anglian Daily Times)

Suffolk Boundaries

Two Counties. The Local Government Act 1888 created the two counties of East Suffolk and West Suffolk, with Bury St Edmunds being the county town of West Suffolk and Ipswich the county town of East Suffolk. This continued 'til 1974

Botesdale. The county boundary went up the middle of Botesdale high street. So one side of Botesdale paid their dues to Ipswich and the other side to Bury St Edmunds.

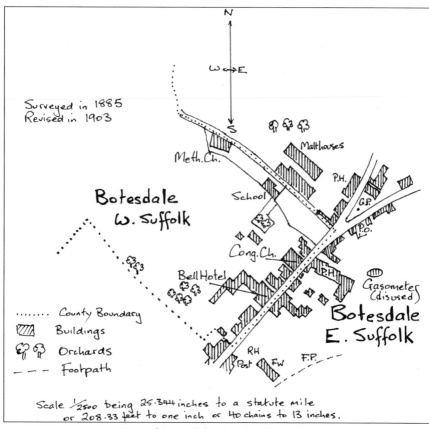

Map of Botesdale showing boundary
(Courtesy of Gale)

Essex parishes were transferred to West Suffolk. Ballingdon-with-Brundon is now part and parcel of Sudbury, and parts of present day Haverhill and Kedington were also part of Essex afore the 1888 Act.

A Broadside and a Near Miss. The Local Government Act 1972 decided that West Suffolk and East Suffolk should merge into the one county of Suffolk (as we know it today), with Ipswich becoming the county town. This occurred in 1974.

Land between Lowestoft and Great Yarmouth was transferred from East Suffolk to Norfolk (How did they cope?).

The near miss? It was also decreed in the '72 Bill that Newmarket and Haverhill would leave West Suffolk and become part of Cambridgeshire, and that Colchester would become a Suffolk town ... but this did not become part of the Act ... phew!

———————

Celtic British Villages. Before the English arrived on our shores, Britain was inhabited by the Celtic Britons, speaking a tongue very similar to Welsh today. That's why Suffolk has four villages with Celtic origins. Iken, settlement of the Iceni (pron Ikeeni), Kenton, farm on the hill (Celt cefn + A-S ton), Monowden, meaning deep wooded valley with clear hill tops, mynydd den, and lastly Clare, thought to be named after its river, which the Romans latinised as *Clarus*.

Norman Place Names. Despite the Normans invading in 1066 and overrunning the place, only four Suffolk villages have a Norman derivation. Boulge (heather covered waste land), Bures (a row of houses), Capel St Andrew (chapel dedicated to St Andrew), and Capel St Mary (chapel dedicated to St Mary).

Remainder of Suffolk villages are either, Anglo-Saxon, Frisian or Viking settlements.

(Courtesy of Barry Chevallier Guild, Aspall Cyder)

The Chevallier Dynasty
(the family behind Aspall Suffolk Cyder)

I think, without fear nor favour, that one of the most historical Suffolk families must be the Chevallier family from Aspall, the leading light in Suffolk cyder and vinegar. But they are not just universally famous for making these delightful intoxicating products. The family history is quite simply amazing.

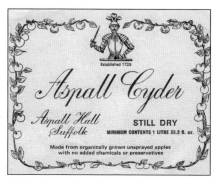

Old Cyder label

Family Tree. The Chevallier family are of Viking stock, and their family tree goes back to the Norse invaders of Northern France, and in particular, Rollo himself, who became the first Duke of Normandy in 911AD, and great great grandfather of William the Conqueror. Hence my statement in the previous paragraph.

Clement Chevallier, 1697 -1762, was the first Chevallier to make cider in 1728. Aspall Cyder are the oldest direct lineage cider makers in the UK.

Clement Chevallier

Reverend Temple Chevallier, 1731 – 1804, featured in the diaries of Arthur Young, Secretary to the Board of Agriculture during his tour of High Suffolk in 1786

Reverend Professor Temple Chevallier, 1794 – 1873, was a famous mathematician and astronomer at Durham University who started the regular study of sun spots and has a crater on the moon named after him.

33

John 'Barley' Chevallier

John Chevallier, (1773/4 –1856), gave his name to Chevallier Barley as its originator. This began as a chance find in 1819 and was systematically developed by John during the 1820s, and valued for outstanding malting qualities and was widely grown during the second half of the nineteenth century; and at one point 75% of all the barley grown worldwide was Chevallier Barley; it's recently been revived.

Frances (Fanny) Anne Chevallier, (1826 – 1864) married Lt Col. Henry Horatio Kitchener in Aspall church. One of their sons later became to be known as Earl Kitchener of Khartoum and Baron of Aspall. The pointing finger of WWI.

'And drink your Aspall Suffolk Cyder too'

Earl Kitchener of Khartoum

John Barrington Chevallier

John Barrington Chevallier (JB), (1857 – 1940) founded Derby County Football Club and played in four FA Cup finals, (won two, lost two). He was the first Chevallier to spell cider with a 'y'. He also exported Aspall Cyder to the officers' mess in India, so that his cousin, Lord Kitchener could still enjoy his Aspall Cyder.

Perronelle Guild

Perronelle Guild (née Chevallier), 1902 – 2003 was one of the first women in England to study agriculture at university. Perronelle was a founder member of the Soil Association in 1946 challenging the orthodoxy of chemical based, intensive agriculture. The Association has today, become an international authority on the principles and practices of organic farming.

Chevallier Street, Ipswich commemorates Dr. Barrington Chevallier, (1818 – 1889) who was the Mayor of Ipswich from 1873 to 1874. He was President of the British Medical Association, East Anglia Branch. He first used Aspall Hall and then The Grove in Ipswich as private asylums.

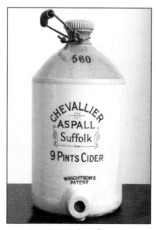

9 pint cider flagon

Cyder for Harrods

All pictures in this section have been supplied by courtesy of Barry Chevallier Guild, Aspall Cyder.

Royal Connections

King Edmund, was crowned in Sudbury on Christmas Day in 855AD. Some say Bures, but I prefer the evidence for Sudbury ... it's more chronological and feasible.

St Edmund for England Badge
(Courtesy of Mark Murphy,
BBC Radio Suffolk)

In 869 AD King Edmund was slain by the Danes and buried in present day Bradfield St Clare (and not Hoxne). Soon after *howsumever*, his body was removed and laid to rest in 'Beodricsworth'. His burial tomb became a popular place of pilgrimage. Edmund's fame grew and grew and eventually he was made a saint. Beodricsworth was renamed St Edmundsbury, meaning a fortified town dedicated to St Edmund (and not meaning the place where St Edmund is buried). He became Patron Saint of England, and remained so, right up to the Crusades. Then he was unceremoniously relegated and St George took over. It's about time we had St Edmund back.

Howsumever, Saint Edmund is still the Patron Saint of Suffolk, (recently made official by Suffolk County Council), and there is still a strong campaign to reinstate him in his rightful position as Patron Saint of England. Who is this George fellow anyway?! This campaign is supported by local MPs, BBC Radio Suffolk, The East Anglian Daily Times, brewers Greene King, and a host more. Please go on-line (st edmund e–petition) and vote to reinstate St Edmund as the rightful patron saint of England.

BBC RADIO SUFFOLK
#EdmundForEngland

BBC Radio Suffolk Sticker
(Courtesy of Mark Murphy,
BBC Radio Suffolk)

Cartoon by Barrie Appleby

Henry **III and the Hemingstone Farter.** It's recorded that in1250AD one Rolland le Pettour (Norman French for 'Farter'), held land in Hemingstone,

Suffolk, by serjeantry. This meant, that instead of paying a rent, the holder would have to annually complete a specific task or act for the king. In this case, Henry III decreed that Rolland le Pettour had to appear before him every Christmas Day, to do a jump, a whistle and a fart (*unum saltum, unum siffletum et unum bumbulum*). This carried on for some years, and by 1330 the eventual holder of this particular serjeantry was referred to as Rolland le Fartere.

Queen Anne. Anne Boleyn's heart is reputed to be buried in a cask at Erwarton Church. Anne's favourite haunt was Erwarton Hall, and she visited her aunt and uncle there on many occasions. So did Henry VIII when he was in amorous pursuit. But later, in different circumstances, Anne Boleyn did say she wanted her heart to be buried at Erwarton Church. After she was beheaded, her heart was ripped out by one of her loyal admirers, and her wishes were carried out (autopsies were rough in *them days*).

Anne Boleyn, Erwarton church
(Courtesy of Wendy Sadler, St Mary's Church, Erwarton)

Mary Tudor, Queen of France, and Henry VIII's favourite sister died in Westhorpe, Suffolk and is laid to rest in St Mary's Church, Bury St Edmunds. Mary had originally been married at the age of 18 to Louis XII of France, who desperately wanted a male heir. However, he was by then 52 and his exertions in the bedchamber with Mary are reputed to have been the cause of his death after only 2 months! Mary later married Charles Brandon 1st Duke of Suffolk and moved to Westhorpe. Henry's famous ship, the *Mary Rose* was named after her, and it's fitting that a very ornate Tudor Rose ceiling is above her resting place today.

James I, brought horse racing to Newmarket and built the first grandstand in 1605. He also built a grand palace for himself and his family in the centre of town.

Charles II, after the Restoration, would also visit Newmarket for several reasons. He initiated an Act of Parliament in 1665 to regulate horse racing under written rules. He also rode horses *hisself* at Newmarket, and his favourite horse was 'Old Rowley', which later became Charles's nickname – hence the 'Rowley Mile' course.

Charles would also hold court in Newmarket twice a year, and his whole entourage would relocate to his palace there. Why else did he visit Newmarket?.......To see a particular voluptuous 'sporting' female called Nell Gwynn, on whom he doted fairly and often (so what do we really mean when we say, 'The Sport of Kings'? Seems pretty popular through the ages which ever 'sport' you choose). There is a Nell Gwynn House in Palace Street.

Prince Albert. Framlingham College was built as a memorial to Prince Albert.

Mrs Simpson and King Edward VIII had a love nest, in 1936 in Felixstowe, at Beach House, Undercliff Road East overlooking the sea. Mrs Simpson, prior to getting divorced from her first husband, stayed here for the necessary six weeks for residential qualification. Edward would arrive in his private plane and land in The Dip on Brackenbury Cliffs, wander off to the nearest pub, buy a few drinks for the locals and then on to Beach House. Mrs Simpson hated Felixstowe in the winter and likened it to Tasmania. Later at Ipswich Assizes Mrs Simpson got her divorce to allow her to marry King Edward VIII. She never returned to Felixstowe.

DON'T HURRY ME – I'M SUFFOLK

Newmarket – Charles II and Nell Gwynn
Cartoon by Barrie Appleby

Lost Suffolk Villages

Over the centuries, especially in mediaeval times, and later in the time of the Tudors and Stuarts, many thousands of villages disappeared throughout the UK. Suffolk too had its fair share, and it's estimated, that perhaps up to 50 to 60 villages have been lost and gone for ever, perhaps even more.

Reasons for lost villages

Firstly through disaster. In mediaeval times, villages were mainly self sufficient and every villager played a role. He or she was an integral part of the village and its well-being. Then, along comes the plague and wipes out a half of the village folk – the village can no longer survive. So they all up and leave and join another village in a similar plight, normally close by, and became a new economic unit. Leaving a lost village behind.

Secondly, especially in Suffolk during the Tudors and Stuarts, the move from decreasing arable farming to more sheep farming. It was less labour intensified and lots of villagers were now out of work. So they moved away, normally to the big towns looking for employment. It had the same effect as the plague on some villages, so once more, they all upped and left to most probably join up with a village in a similar situation. Leaving a lost village behind.

Thirdly, and perhaps the most callous and cruel, were the results of emparking, especially during the 1700s and 1800s when men made vast fortunes from the colonies and wanted to buy themselves instant gentrification. The lord of the manor could be looking out of his window across the meadows down to the shore, thinking about the panorama. Only for the M'Lady to say, 'Pity about that village down there ... spoiling the view.' Emparking would be the answer. Villages were demolished and uprooted to enhance the view from the manor house, the great hall, or the 'big house'.

Fourthly, in Suffolk, we have seen villages lost to the sea. Some have gone forever, and others are just a relic of previous halcyon days. Even the larger villages and towns have suffered ... Half of old Aldeburgh is buried under the sea or eroded away.

Last but not least, where villages have been swallowed up by town expansion. But invariably the place name has remained as a part of the town (like Ingate becoming part of Beccles) – I have included some of these in my list.

Slaughden, c1900, before the storms
(Courtesy of Suffolk Record Office, Ipswich. Ref K681/1/3/83)

Slaughden after the storms
(Courtesy of Suffolk Record Office, Ipswich. Ref K681/1/3/86)

The following are some of these lost Suffolk villages, many of which have been kept alive through Suffolk surnames.

Alston	Now part of Trimley St Martin
Applethwaite	Lost. Believed to have been just north east of Norton
Brewington	Lost. Believed to have been in East Suffolk
Bulcamp	Now part of Blythburgh
Creeting St Olave	Now part of Creeting St Mary
Dunningworth or **Dunningham**	Now part of Tunstall
Felchurch	Now part of Washbrook
Gallington	From a lost village in Suffolk – whereabouts unknown
Grimsey	Lost. Somewhere along the River Stour - Grimes Eye
Hallowtree	Now part of Nacton
Hazelwood	Now part of Aldeburgh
Little Bricett	Now part of Offton
Little Fakenham	Now part of Euston
Little Redisham	Now part of Ringsfield
Loudham	Now part of Petistree
Lymborne	Now in South Elmham
Pilborough/ Pilburgh	Lost. From a village somewhere in the Bosmere Hundred
Rampley/ Rampling	From a lost village in Suffolk, whereabouts unknown
Riddleston(e)	Lost. Somewhere in the Polstead area on top of a hill.
Scotchmere	Lost. Somewhere north of Bury St Edmunds by a lake
Stallworthy	Lost 13th century village. Pronounced Stollery by the locals
Slaughden	Lost. Immediately south of Aldeburgh – once a thriving port

Thorpe	Now part of Ashfield
Thurleston	Now part of Whitton
Walton	Now part of Felixstowe

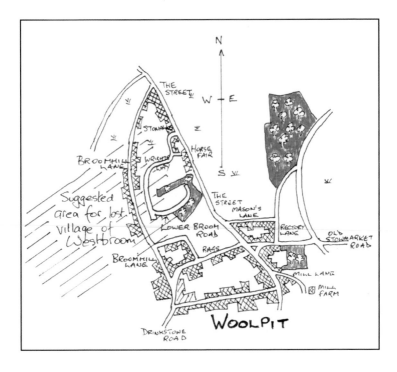

Suggested area of Westbroom
(Courtesy of Gale)

Westbroom	Now part of Woolpit.
Wiston	Now part of Wissington. But Wiston was original settlement
Wortham Southmoor	Now part of Wortham St Mary
Wortham Everard	Also part of Wortham St Mary
Woolby	Lost Suffolk Viking hamlet – *wolf* plus *by* (fortified hill)

Suffolk Towns and Villages

Aldeburgh. Suffolk has the annual world famous 'Aldeburgh Festival'. But it's not held in Aldeburgh – it's held at Snape Maltings – and guess what? Snape Maltings aren't in Snape – they're in the next village – Tunstall.

The Moot Hall in Aldeburgh used to be in the centre of town a mile from the sea.

Bawdsey Manor was bought in 1936 for £24,000 to establish a research station for developing the Chain Home RDF radar system.

Blythburgh is sometimes called Bulcamp by the older locals – it was included in the Blythburgh parish boundaries, and means 'battleground'; the scene of a battle in 645AD between the ill-fated East Anglian King Anna, and the victorious Danish King Penda of Mercia. King Anna and his son were both buried in Blythburgh Church.

Boxford has the oldest recorded working garage in Europe, as well as the oldest recorded shop in England.

Bradfield Combust is so called because it had a great fire, when the granary barns were set alight in 1329 during the Peasants' Revolt. They were objecting to the wealth of the Abbey at Bury St Edmunds, so decided to set fire to the Abbey's granary at Bradfield.

Brandon. Flints mined at Brandon were the finest in the world for flintlocks. They were exported all over the known world, even the USA. Therefore, Wild Bill Hickock, Davey Crockett and Daniel Boone, would have all used Suffolk flints.

Bury St Edmunds is known as 'The Cradle of the Law'. In 1214, the English barons secretly and deliberately met in the Abbey, wanting inspiration from Saint Edmund. They certainly got it. They drafted the Magna Carta, the cornerstone of English liberty.
Hence Bury's town motto, 'Shrine of a King, Cradle of the Law'
King John signed it a year later at Runnymede in 1215.

Dalham. The ornate wrought iron gates at Dalham Hall were crafted by two local blacksmiths, one of whom was called Tubal Cain Alecock. The

first bender of iron (blacksmith), in the Old Testament, is also called Tubal Cain.

Debenham has a 'Groaning Stone'. Said to be at the true source of the River Deben where legend says the ancient Celts had a throne, and indeed, some say the East Angles did as well. On a full moon the stone is said to move and moan at midnight.

Dunwich used to be the capital town of the East Angles.

It's also the birthplace of John Day, b.1522AD, who was the first printer to use an Anglo-Saxon type set, which he invented.

'The Ship Inn' at Dunwich was the first public house to be licensed.

King John awarded Dunwich its first Royal Charter. This meant, that many many years later, it could become a 'Rotten Borough', and entitled Dunwich to have two MPs during the early 1800s in our early 'democratic system'.

Eastbridge. The Eel's Foot public house is believed to be so called, because of the old way East Suffolkers used to say 'devil'. They supposedly pronounced it as 'deveel' and therefore, 'Eel's Foot' is short for 'deveel's foot'.

Ipswich is the oldest recorded English town, and the first settlement built by the English invaders, the 'Angles', in the 5th century, after the Romans had left.

Lord Horatio Nelson in 1800 became High Steward of Ipswich. It is also believed that he and Lady Hamilton spent nights together at the 'Great White Horse Hotel'

Martlesham Heath was first used as an airfield by the Royal Flying Corps during WWI. In 1917 it also became an experimental airbase, test flying all sorts of aircraft all over East Suffolk. This was a highly dangerous job since most of the aircraft were delivered to Martlesham by different, small manufacturers, and the first job of the R.A.F. was to see whether the planes would actually fly at all. In 1939 it became a WWII airfield and Group Captain Sir Douglas Bader, the famous WWII fighter pilot, who had both legs amputated, flew from RAF Martlesham. There is a local hostelry which bears his name.

Newmarket is a town in Suffolk. But … if you want to visit another Suffolk town by road from Newmarket, you cannot do so unless you go into Cambridgeshire.

Newmarket is so called because Exning had the plague. Exning was the main market town in the area along the Icknield Way. But in the 1200s the plague hit Exning and the market was disbanded. A new market was set up just down the road – Newmarket

Newmarket Racecourse is mainly in Cambridgeshire. The Rowley Mile starts in Cambridgeshire and finishes in Suffolk. The July Course is wholly across the border.

Eels Foot pub sign

Orford Ness is the longest bar spit in the UK and the best maintained one in Europe.

It was used as a research centre in both World Wars, and saw the initial radar breakthrough. The Atomic Weapons Research Establishment had a base here, and the buildings can still be seen today – it closed in 1973. Later in the 70s it became a radio transmitting centre, including the BBC World Service from Sept 1982 to March 2011. It closed in 2012 and the island is now owned by the National Trust. Access is still limited because of the delicate and fragile state of the natural environment.

Pakenham. Only English village with two working mills, one wind one water.

Polstead Blacks are edible cherries only grown in Polstead and nowhere else.

Shotley Peninsular is the last place in England where outbreaks of the bubonic plague were recorded, from 1906 to 1918.

Slaughden used to be Suffolk's busiest seaport. The Martello Tower is the most northerly UK tower, and the only one which is clover shaped.

Kippperdrome
(Courtesy of Jenny Hursell and Paul Scriven, Southwold Museum)

Inhabitants of Slaughden were called, 'Cod Bangers'. They had specially built boats, (in the Slaughden boatyards), with a uniquely designed well that kept the fish alive 'til they came ashore. The fisher folk would then kill the fish, one at a time with a cudgel, hence they were called 'Cod Bangers'.

Sole is the *owd* way of saying Southwold – hence Sole Bay (Southwold Bay).

Southwold's old fish market down by the harbour used to be called the 'Kipperdrome', due to the shape of the building – now demolished and a caravan park.

Stoke by Clare Church has the oldest church clock in the country with the original mechanism, and was deliberately designed with just the one hand – the hour hand.

Stowmarket – John Curwen, an assistant minister at Stowmarket Congregational Church, adapted Sarah Glover's method of teaching sight singing. He used the 'Doh, Ray, Me, Fah, Soh, Lah, Te, Doh' method, to teach young people at church to sing. If he hadn't have done this, we would have been one song short in *The Sound of Music*.

Walberswick Ferry, operated by ferrywoman Dani Church, is the fifth generation of her family to operate the ferry since 1885. Dani is proud to carry on the traditions of her family, and refuses to use an outboard motor. I have used the ferry many times, and Dani has stated quite often, that by rowing, she can eat and drink as much as she likes, and stay fit. I also remember her Dad, who was also an interesting character, with a very dry, Suffolk sense of humour.

Woodbridge, was formerly a large shipbuilding centre. Sir Francis Drake's flagship, 'The Pelican', was built in Woodbridge. At sea he renamed it 'The Golden Hind' in December 1577, and circum-navigated the world. He was the first Englishman to do so.

The Walberswick Ferry c.1900 (Courtesy of Jenny Hursell and Paul Scriven, Southwold Museum)

Owd Suffolkers

Bird. Rev Brian Bird was the first vicar to bring jazz bands and skiffle groups into the church. St Bartholomew's, Groton, was the first church to hold jazz and skiffle concerts in the UK, including all time greats like Chris Barber, Acker Bilk and Lonnie Donnegan. The 'with it' Rev also writ a book on the history of skiffle and also had his own jazz band.

'I also christened the author – a long time ago!'

(Courtesy of The Windmill House Collection)

Brian Bird was also an activist and took on Dr. Beeching in the early 1960's. He led and organised the protests, and he saved Sudbury railway station and the Sudbury to Marks Tey railway line from the 'Beeching Axe'.

Bradman. Charles Andrew Bradman was born in 1832 in Withersfield, Suffolk. He emigrated to Australia in 1852 to N.S.W. He was grandfather to Sir Donald Bradman, the greatest cricketer the world has ever seen. On his last tour to England, Sir Don visited Withersfield. The pub there is a cricketing shrine with much memorabilia in one devoted corner.

Garrett. Dr Elizabeth Garrett, 1836 to 1917, was an absolute first. The first English female to qualify as a physician and surgeon in Britain. The co-founder of the first hospital staffed by women. The first dean of a British medical school. The first female in Britain to be elected to a school board. The first female mayor, when she became Mayoress of Aldeburgh in 1908. First female magistrate in Britain. It's quite fitting that a wing of Ipswich Hospital is named after her.

Leman. Sir John Leman from Beccles became Lord Mayor of London in 1616. In his will he created a free school, for a number of boys in Beccles and from an adjoining village. And you might not believe this ... he also included boys from one other village (Gillingham) ... just north of the River Waveney ... from Norfolk ... so he wasn't prejudiced. There is still a school in Beccles named after him today.

Suckling. Catherine Suckling was a young lady from Barsham, Suffolk, who married a rector from Norfolk, the Rev. Edmund Nelson. Yes! ! ! She was Lord Nelson's mum. Therefore Nelson is half Suffolk ! ! ! No wonder he was more than half tidy. Does that mean to say that a 'half nelson' is all Suffolk?

Tyler. Wat Tyler, leader of the Peasants' Revolt in 1381, came from Suffolk. Recent documentation which has come to light shows Wat Tyler to have been born and bred in Hadleigh, Suffolk.

Tyrell. Sir James Tyrell is the nasty Suffolk man who supported King Richard III. And on the King's instructions, he reputedly murdered the Princes in The Tower in 1483.

After Richard III came Henry VII, and he brought Sir James to justice by torturing him to get a confession. Tyrell was beheaded at Tower Hill in 1502, and the truth of the matter died with him.

Little Suffolk Oddities

Avocet. The British wading bird, the avocet, was on the verge of extinction. So much so, that it had disappeared all together, and hadn't been seen for some time. Thought to be lost and gone for ever. Then ... One day on the Suffolk coast they were spotted. They had returned. With lots of careful management and monitoring the numbers have been steadily increasing. This wonderful encouraging story is why the avocet is the logo for the RSPB.

Avocet on RSPB logo

British Museum. Three of the top ten British Treasures at the British Museum, are from the county of Suffolk. We have the top billing with the number one spot, plus numbers five and eight. Namely. The Sutton Hoo burial site, the Mildenhall Treasure and the Hoxne Hoard. Shows how important Suffolk is in the evolution of this England.

BT discovered Broadband at Martlesham, Suffolk. But where is Broadband in Suffolk now? We're still waiting!

Cutty Wren. Middleton in East Suffolk is believed to be the last place in Britain where the ancient ritual of 'Cutty Wren' takes place. This traditional ceremony goes back to Neolithic times, and has recently become an annual event with a wooden 'wren' at its centre on St Stephens Day, 26th December. During the ritual 'The Bell' inn at Middleton plays an important part. Oh Yes!

Cutty Wren at The Bell, Middleton 2003,
with Old Glory Molly Dancers and Musicianers
(Courtesy of Old Glory Molly [the original])

Dutch Cartographers were employed in the 1700s to make maps of England more detailed, and they were paid by the letter. So what did they do? They added letters on to earn more money. So Edwardston became Edwardstone and Drinkston became Drinkstone, and there are many more examples. Having said that, the locals still pronounce the village names as they should be … prior to the Dutch additions.

Greene King. Mr Greene and Mr King, joint partners in the famous Bury St Edmunds' brewery parted company over a very big issue in the mid 1800s. Mr. Greene was anti-slavery and Mr. King was pro-slavery. And in

fact, Mr. Greene's daughter went on to marry Thomas Clarkson, the anti-slavery campaigner.

Halesworth Police Murder. Victorian policeman Ebeneezer Tye was murdered in Halesworth in 1862. John Ducker, also a Halesworth man, was arrested and tried. He was found guilty and became the last man to be hanged in public in Suffolk. 1863

Martello Towers, which dot the Suffolk coast, are so called because they copy the design of the Mortello Tower in Corsica. The English fleet pounded Mortello Point in Corsica, prior to the Napoleonic Wars in 1794. The English were unsuccessful and withdrew. But we were so impressed with the tower, that it was copied in our own defence against Napoleon, 1805 to 1815.

Orwell River. Eric Arthur Blair, the famous novelist and journalist, was so inspired with one little corner of Suffolk, he used it in his pen name, George Orwell.

Sizewell Gap. During the mid 1700s and early 1800s, Sizewell Gap was rife with tea smuggling. It has been reported, that even during the day, up to 100 carts and 300 horses could be seen on the beach loaded with tea. Tea was taxed at 119% and very expensive, so smuggling was the answer. Up to 80% of tea consumed in England was contraband. Suffolk had its share of tea smugglers including the notorious Hadleigh Gang who were some 60 in number, and regular visitors to Sizewell Gap. The Wright Gang also occupied themselves in this illicit trade.

There is an old Suffolk dialect word for a parcel of smuggled tea, *a dallop*. It varied in quantity, from 6 to 16 pounds, and perhaps could even be more.

Toby Walks in Blythburgh. So called, because in 1750, 'Black Toby' was hanged for a crime he didn't commit. He was a Black soldier in the Dragoons, and after a night of drinking was found next morning, lying alongside the serving girl, who lay dead. She was unscathed, totally unmarked or scratched, but dead. The people strung Black Toby up, but he still comes back to haunt the very spot.

The Suffolk Revolution

Suffolk was the powerhouse behind the Agrarian Revolution in its early years and throughout time since. The mechanisation of agricultural farming was also the forerunner of what became known as the Industrial Revolution.

A wooden AY plough circa 1845
Line drawing by Barrie Appleby

1778   Garretts of Leiston were founded and became a world leader.

1789   Ransomes of Ipswich were founded and also led the world.

c.1799   Garretts invented the 'Horse Hoe' and their 'Lever Corn Drill' and started to export them all round the world.

1800   James Smyth from a little Suffolk village called Peasenhall invented the Suffolk Lever Drill, which made drilling seed easier and more economical and he also perfected the Lever Horse Hoe.

1803   Ransomes produced the self sharpening chilled cast iron plough share. This was accidentally invented when some molten iron spilled on the cold factory floor and cooled quickly. Chilled cast iron was stumbled upon quite literally. The Ransomes dynasty was built on an accident.

1806 Garretts built the first ever 'Horse Power Threshing Machine' which would radically change threshing time, and be the inspiration for the steam driven threshers, later invented by ... yes you've guessed it, by Garretts.

1808 Ransomes patented standardisation of plough parts. This particular act along with their 1803 invention, revolutionised farming worldwide, and Ransomes became a leading contender in that global market, having already become Britain's largest plough and agricultural equipment manufacturer.

1832 Ransomes were the first company to manufacture a cylinder lawn mower. Though designed by Edwin Budding, Ransomes held a licence for its production. Not only did it revolutionise gardening, but also sport.. . more games could be played on grass, and led to a phenomenal rise in rugby, cricket, lawn tennis, football etc etc.

Garrett's Stand at Great Exhibition, 1851
(Courtesy of Anna Mercer, Long Shop Museum, Leiston)

1838 James Smyth Jnr invented the Suffolk Corn Drill, which was the forerunner of others to copy, and it put the name of Smyth on the international map.

1840 Garretts produced a set of steam threshing machinery. These became so popular they were exported throughout the world. Such was the demand for steam engines and threshers from the Leiston Works, that Garretts couldn't cope in their existing works, so they started the first mass production line in the world.

1842 Ransomes of Ipswich demonstrated the first self moving steam engine at the Royal Agricultural Society's Show – The traction engine.

1867 Ransomes produced a hand powered lawnmower, and called it 'Automoton'

Garretts, Ransomes, Smyth, Sims, and Jeffreys are pioneering names synonymous with Suffolk and agricultural machinery. Not only in Suffolk, but throughout the world. Not only in the 1800s, but through the ages to the present day.

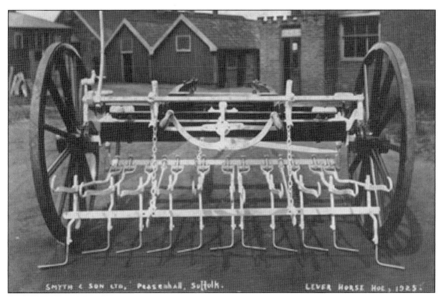

(Courtesy of Lisa Harris, Museum of East Anglian Life. Ref: STMEA.A.1399)

Mullett's Farm, Buxhall, Suffolk, c.1900
(Courtesy of Lisa Harris, Museum of East Anglian Life. Ref: STMEA.SPS1867)

Advertisement for Horse Boots
(Courtesy of Alan Riddleston)

And what about the present day? The names may have changed, and the changes renamed, but we still have Suffolk inventors manufacturing Suffolk inventions in Suffolk, still exporting to foreign climes. And one in particular is in the eccentric mould, and fits in well in a chapter about curious facts in the Curious County.

Garretts is now a living museum of a past era in Leiston. Their Long Shop Museum is an absolute must to visit, just to re-live the atmosphere of a bygone age.

Ransomes are still on the go in their specialised field of turf maintenance and care, and are still coming up with new concepts and improvements.

But what about the new boys on the block?

Claydon Seed Drills at Wickhambrook near Newmarket, are best described as inventive farmers. They have built up a well respected reputation worldwide, for the manufacture of farming equipment and the 'Claydon System'. Part of this system is the remarkable Claydon Seed Drill, which is so simple in its concept that it's brilliant, enabling farmers to maximise usage with minimum tillage drilling. It is absolutely true to say that Claydons are ground breaking in their field.

Richard Western Trailers in Framlingham also have a well respected international reputation. They bring modern day technology in today's farming. This can be seen particularly well in their Suffolk Trailer and their grain chasers. They also concentrate on many other specialist trailers, and produce a commodity that Suffolk can be proud of.

Shellbourne and Reynolds at Stanton, right in the heart of Suffolk, also lead the way. They export to Australia, the USA and more. The one thing perhaps they are most famous for, is inventing a stripper header as an attachment on a combine harvester. It strips the ears off the standing corn, so only the ears go through the combine and not unwanted straw. It therefore increases the throughput by decreasing the amount put through.

Incidentally, a very curious fact is ... it was actually the Romans that invented this concept. They had a set of stripper fingers mounted on the front edge of a low wagon, which was pushed by bullocks at the rear, and the ears of corn fell into the wagon.

Suffolk's Extraordinary Engineer

Jordan ATV Engineering deserves a section all on its own, and is well in keeping with the modern agrarian revolution. Jordan ATV Engineering is a little company, and a Suffolk gem. It's very unique, and is run by an eccentric Suffolk inventive engineer, Jerv Jordan, just outside Sudbury. Jerv also commentates at various shows, including the prestigious Suffolk Show, on vintage tractors and other farming equipment and machinery. He

Jerv Jordan

Jerv's Mate Fred – (similar looks but no good at welding!)

has a style all of his own, which is very pleasing to the ear, and at times, extremely humorous and funny.

Jerv has spent a lifetime in agricultural machinery in one way or another. He was born into it and followed in his father's footsteps. Engineering oil, radiator coolants and diesel fluid run through Jerv's veins. Everything was getting bigger and bigger, huge and ginormous; Jerv saw a niche and a need in the market. There appeared a vacancy for small farming machinery being drawn by ATVs (all terrain vehicles ... or quad bikes).

Farmers were being encouraged to leave margins round the outside of their fields to encourage wildlife, flora and fauna. These areas of nature would be best maintained with small machinery rather than huge. Laying down cover for game birds is also more economically done with smaller machinery ... there are many more examples.

Jordan ATV Engineering responded and built the world's first purpose built ATV seeder. Jerv has made updated versions ever since and they have been sold throughout the UK, in parts of Europe and further afield. Another first, was the patented side arm verge mower for ATVs. All Jerv's creations are named after Arthurian characters ... one of his little idiosyncrasies.

Super Sow – Lite ATV Seed Drill

Another first was Jerv responding to people with certain disabilities. He designed an adjustable tripod swivel seat with a back rest, especially for disabled people who wanted to pursue country sports. This simple invention allowed disabled anglers to go fishing without falling over into the river, especially when they were casting out. It also allowed disabled people to take part in clay pigeon shooting without toppling over at the crucial time when pulling the trigger, or being bowled over backwards, after they had. It has also spilled out into other uses, and has allowed a college lecturer, who became disabled, to continue lecturing in his usual animated style.

Another first? Jerv is determined to take the World Tractor Land Speed Record off the Americans, and bring it back to the UK. He has found a backer and a sponsor and is preparing for an attempt in 2014. He is modifying the tractor *hisself*.

During his limited spare time, you'll see Jerv playing blues harp with various blues bands at Suffolk buskers' nights and jamming sessions. He's a wonderful Suffolk eccentric who would go well with Rex Garrod … I can't pay a higher compliment.

Never too busy to pose

Finished Job

All photos in this section are courtesy of The Jerv Jordan Collection

Dolphin's Dart

Lesley Dolphin, the charismatic and popular BBC Radio Suffolk producer and presenter of the Afternoon Show, has a few little oddities. 'Why?' You may well ask. Every weekday, Lesley runs the 'Dolphin's Dart' competition, whereby certain clues are given out, on air, about a particular Suffolk

Lesley Dolphin
(Courtesy BBC Radio Suffolk)

village. This is the village where 'Dolphin's Dart' has landed. Listeners ring in and guess the name, and are invited to talk about the village, and to give some interesting facts. Here are just a few:

Beck Row. The airfield at Mildenhall was the site of an amazing spectacle in October 1934 when it was officially dedicated by King George V. It was the start of the Royal Aero Clubs', England to Australia, air race. Some 70,000 people gathered to watch both events. Twenty aircraft took off and it was won by two Englishmen, Black and Scott who completed the flight to Melbourne in under 17 hours and created a new record.

Coney Weston. There is a penny whistle on the village sign because it was invented here by farm labourer Robert Clarke. He went into business producing them and ended up rich enough to buy up the farm he worked on. The whistles are still made and sold around the world but these days they are produced in Kent. Apparently the 2013 Eurovision winner, Denmark, used a Clarke tin whistle!!

Robert Clark on Coney Weston Village Sign
(Courtesy of The Windmill Collection)

Henstead. The most unusual place in this village must be the exotic garden! It's been created by Andrew Brogan who has used over 70 tons of rock and over 100 large palm trees. The backbone of the garden is a series of buildings including a tropical style summerhouse and Thai pavilion. There is a Lord of the Rings style composting toilet. There are fish filled ponds, water lilies, streams and waterfalls. It's open every Wednesday from 8th May.

Hinderclay. The Church in Hinderclay, St Mary's is probably most famous for its ***gotch***. This is an old Suffolk dialect word for a large pitcher. Here, it was used to hold beer when the bellringers got thirsty. The inscription on the *gotch* is dated 25th March 1724, which in those times, would have been New Year's Day.

Huntingfield. The most amazing thing about Huntingfield is the ceiling in St. Mary's church. In the 19th century, Mrs Mildred Holland, the vicar's wife, spent 7 years lying on her back … at the top of scaffolding, painting the ceiling of the church with angels, saints, gold gilding and lettering. Her work was recorded in a diary by her husband the Reverend William Holland. It is truly an amazing sight.

Finningham. The year 2013 is the year they brought back **The Pie Powder Fair**. It used to be an annual event held on the village green when locals would gather and have a good time. But it was also an event where servants and labourers could be hired, and a court was held to try vagrants and other people of no fixed abode. These itinerants were known as *Pied Poudre* (French for dusty feet), hence the title of the fair! They don't intend to do any more hiring or trying, but aim to give everyone a good time.

Hartest. On the green in Hartest is a large granite boulder commemorating a famous treaty. The War of the Spanish Succession raged until nearly every state of Western Europe was drawn in, and by 1713, the long struggle had almost exhausted Europe including England. The hero of the war was John Churchill, Duke of Marlborough, who was the victor of many battles with the French, including Blenheim in 1704. On April 11th 1713, the Treaty of Utrecht was signed, and England gained Gibraltar, Minorca, Newfoundland and territorial rights in Canada.

July 7th was appointed as a day of general thanksgiving throughout England, and Hartest was not backward in participating in the general joy of the people. A great stone, which lay in a field near Somerton common, was to be the memorial to the treaty. A sledge was specially constructed, and all the neighbouring farmers lent their horses to draw the huge mass to the village. Forty horses were harnessed to the sledge, and with a trumpeter mounted on the top of the stone, the procession triumphantly proceded to Hartest, where the stone was placed in its present position, and where it has remained until its commemorative interest has been almost forgotten. But not now.

A 300 year anniversary event was held on Hartest Green to celebrate the placing of the Stone on the Green on 7th July 1713, including a re-enactment of the stone making its way from Somerton to Hartest.

Melton. Edwin Lankester, born in Melton in April 1814, was a surgeon and naturalist who made a major contribution to the control of cholera in London. He was the first public analyst in England. He eventually became the first Medical Officer for Health and his microscopical examination of water is still today one of the standard tests for testing the quality of drinking water.

Monk Soham. Claude Morley was born here. He was a respected entomologist who specialised in Hymenoptera and Diptera (bees, wasps,

Edwin Lankester of Melton

ants and sawflies!). His collection fills 260 drawers at the Ipswich museum. When Dolphin's Dart landed here in 2010, Joy Pipe rang in because she could remember being paid a shilling by Mr. Morley for a huge beetle she'd found.

Redgrave. Burial vaults have been discovered under the floor of St. Mary's church. The vaults were discovered in the 1930's and then they were lost again until 2011, when Kathy Mills dislodged a flagstone as she was rehearsing very enthusiastically for a production of Quasimodo! The vault was opened for the public to have a look – since then it's been resealed. Members of the family still live here.

Snape. JK Rowling took the village name of Snape for one of the characters in her Harry Potter stories. He is Severus Snape, the potions master, the Head of Slytherin and the converted Death Eater. What is it about Snape that inspired such a character?

Stradishall. Cake maker Jane Asher lived here. The poet James Thompson, who wrote the words to Rule Britannia, is also associated with the village.

Sweffling. Gavin, who was born in the village in the 1940's, told us that radio presenter, Wilfred Pickles, had once referred to the village of Sweffling, as the Monte Carlo of Suffolk … as it had only one bright light.

CHAPTER 4

Suffolk Surnames
M to Z

This follows on from my previous book, 'Sloightly on the Sosh', where we had an explanation of surnames, why we have surnames, the different types of surnames, what they mean, and why some surnames are peculiarly Suffolk. It included a list of surnames, A to L, that are Suffolk and Suffolk only. It's only natural to complete the alphabet and include M to Z in 'Don't Hurry Me – I'm Suffolk'.

Once again, I would like to thank BBC Radio Suffolk, BBC Radio Suffolk listeners and of course, Lesley Dolphin. Lesley is one of BBC Radio Suffolk's presenters, and whose idea it was for me to include Suffolk surnames in a book. This idea came out on air during my weekly 'Haylock's Half Hour for Forty Minutes' with Lesley, when we were getting such a fantastic listener response regarding their surnames.

Howsumever, I have received many e-mails, phone calls and letters from a number of people complaining that their surname is not in my Suffolk list, although they can trace their family back to the year dot, and have always been based in Suffolk. It's hard to explain sometimes, that the family might be Suffolk through and through, but the surname isn't. For example, a family with the surname of Smith or Taylor might be able to trace their family tree back to the 1200s or even earlier, and have always been recorded in Suffolk. This would make them Suffolk families, but not with a Suffolk surname. Smith and Taylor are widely dispersed throughout England.

It is also worth recording, that these two books, 'Don't Hurry Me – I'm Suffolk' and 'Sloightly on the Sosh', are the only places where you will find a written recording of Suffolk surnames, other than on my website, www.charliehaylock.com

There are dictionaries of English surnames, and websites showing surname distributions, and even documents showing the different surnames in Suffolk and other counties. But nowhere, other than these two books, will you find a list of surnames that are peculiarly Suffolk, and Suffolk only.

I have taken the 1881 census and before as my benchmark. After that date, due to two world wars and an increase in global travel, surnames are starting to become more widespread. I feel therefore, it is essential, that we have these surnames with Suffolk roots recorded, before they become lost in an English surname stew.

Matilda Makejoy
Christmas 1296

'The twelve year old Prince Edward gave two shillings to the famous acrobatic dancer, Matilda Makejoy. She made her vaults, almost certainly naked, before the Lord Edward, the King's son, at Ipswich in 1296. Matilda was still performing for Edward at Christmas in 1311 when he was 27 and King.'

M

Makejoy   Anglo-Saxon nickname for someone who makes joy – could be a court jester or court 'entertainer'
Maliphant   Norman French for naughty child – *mal enfant*
Malvenue   Norman French for someone who committed a bad crime or act
Manwin   Anglo-Saxon for servant friend / man friend
Marjoram   Norman French for the herb *marjerane* or *marjeram* – a grower or seller of herbs BUT most likely a herbalist.
Marking   Old English – Mary kin – family of Mary
Markwell   Anglo-Saxon – someone who lives by the source of the river on a boundary line. Another Suffolk alternative is **Markle**
Maxim   Son of Maggs, pet form of Margaret. The 'ggs' often got *writ* down as 'x'. Other variations – Moxon, Moxom and Maxam – these are not Suffolk

Archibald Alfred Maxim aged 14
Training Ship Warspite 1902

Alice, Lilian and Rosina Maxim
circa 1898 Stanstead, Suffolk

Courtesy of Patricia Winfield
Granddaughter of Archibald Alfred

Mayhew   Old French – Norman form of Matthew
Meekins   Meekin literally means the family of Mayhew. And Meekins means son of Meekin. Another Suffolk alternative is Making
Mayse   Another Suffolk variation of the surname – Son of May (Mayhew)
Moye   Another Suffolk variation and the Suffolk pronunciation of May – Son of May (Mayhew) Moye
Melding   Someone from Milden Suffolk
Melford   Someone from Long Melford
Mendham   Someone from Mendham
Morling   *Moor* is Anglo-Saxon, not just for moor, but also for fen or marsh. *Ling* is Anglo-Saxon for son of, young of, or followers of. Therefore, we have the son of a dweller by the fen or marsh

Mendham Village sign
(Courtesy of The Windmill Collection)

Arthur & Charlie Morling
(Courtesy of Kath Whiting
[nee Morling])

Lily Morling,
Eel's Foot, Landlady 1927 to 1944
(Courtesy of Keith Morling)

Morphew This is a Suffolk variation of Morfey. A Norman name, *Mal Fe* meaning Bad Faith and originally was a term of abuse given to the Saracens or the devil – later – someone who's Ill-omened, – lots of bad luck – bedevilled

Mothersole Anglo-Saxon – *modig sawol* – meaning brave proud soul OR an oath name *Modhers Sawol* – by my mother's soul

Motte Norman-French – Someone who lives on or at a fortified hill, *motte*

Mouser Anglo-Saxon nickname for someone behaving like a mouse – timid and shy OR the complete opposite – brash and gregarious. *Howsumever* could also refer to a pest controller

Mower Anglo-Saxon – *mawan* – to mow – a mower

Oscar Mothersole
(Courtesy of
Miss Maureen Mothersole)

71

Mutimer, Father and Son, working in Debenham
(Courtesy of John Mutimer)

Mullenger Norman French *molinier* for miller

Munnings Anglo-Saxon – *Munding* means son of Munda – Munda means protector

Musk First recorded as Geoffrey Morch which is the Anglo-Saxon pronunciation and the Viking pronunciation is *musk* – It literally means the younger son

Mutimer Suffolk variation of Mortimer – from Mortemer (Seine-Inferieure)

Muttit French Huguenot name derives from *mottet* a small fortified hill

Muttock Suffolk variation of Maddock and Mattock – A pre 7th century personal name from Celtic origins, either Breton, Cornish, or Welsh – derives from *matoc* or *madawc* meaning the goodly one.

Ada Maude Muttitt
(Courtesy of Paul Stockdale)

N

Nesling	Anglo-Saxon for nestling, a young bird too young to leave the nest … a child. Or Anglo-Saxon *nestlian*, to make a nest or home
Nickles	Suffolk variation of Nicholas – appears in the 1086 Domesday Book. Comes from the Greek – meaning 'Victory People' – a common Medieval name. First recording of Nickles is in the 1783 Suffolk Pipe Rolls
Noller	Originally – atten Alder – dweller by the alders – later pronounced atte Nolder – later as Noller
Noy	A Hebrew name derives from Noah – meaning long life

O

Orford	Someone from Orford.
Orris	Comes from the Latin 'Horatius', a Roman family name. Came over to England during the Renaissance from Italy 14th to 17th century. **Oris** and **Orriss** are also Suffolk variations
Ortis	Norman French – someone from Artois France
Orvis	Suffolk variation of office or officer – Norman French *orfreis* meaning a dealer in orphrey or gold embroidery
Ours	Suffolk variation of Owers – Anglo-Saxon for dweller near a bank or steep slope
Outlaw	Viking name *utlagi* – pronounced outlaw
Oxfoot	Anglo-Saxon for ox foot – nickname for someone with large feet

P

Pakenham	from Pakenham Suffolk
Papillon	Norman French, *papillon* meaning butterfly – inconsistent
Pannifer	Anglo-Saxon for *penig foeder* – penny father – a miser
Pattle	A Suffolk variation of Middle English beadle, originally a minor parish official in the English church

Viking Outlaw

Perebourne
Anglo-Saxon nickname – pear brown – a swarthy complexion

Perkinson Suffolk variation of Parkinson – son of Perkin or Parkyn which in itself means son of or family of Pierre

Pettingale Son of the Portuguese – From the Middle English word Portingale meaning 'from Portugal'

Pickers Anglo-Saxon for maker or seller of pikes or pick axes

Pickess same as Pickers above – maker or seller of pikes or pick axes

Pilborough From a lost Suffolk village, Pileburgh in the Bosmere Hundred – Anglo-Saxon *Pileberga*, Also shown as **Pilbow** and **Pilbrow**

Pinner Someone who makes pins – big wooden pins for joining, especially boat building

Pintel Anglo-Saxon for the male reproductive organ – very rare name

Pipe A piper

Plampin Norman French origin *blanc pain*, white bread – a baker

Edward Plampin
(Courtesy of David Bartholomew)

Playford   From Playford

Pleasants   Suffolk variation of Pleasance Norman French *plaisance* – meaning pleasant and usually referred to a female

Posford   From Potsford Barn, Letheringham, Wickham Market

Powling   Suffolk variation of Paulin – Meaning son of Paul

Pritty   Anglo-Saxon *preatigg* for crafty and cunning

Pulfer   Anglo-Saxon *pulver* for one who grinds powders – at first for medicinal purposes, but later it also meant gunpowder.

Pung   Anglo-Saxon *pung* meaning purse or pouch – a maker of purses and pouches.

R

Raker   Suffolk variation of the surname Rake or Raikes. Anglo-Saxon name for someone who lives in a narrow valley from *hraca* meaning throat – narrow valley shaped like a throat.

Rampley   From a lost Suffolk village. Sometimes as **Rampling**

Rattell   Suffolk diminutive of the name Ratt – son of Ratt – Anglo-Saxon *raet* – would refer to a rat catcher – therefore son of a ratcatcher

Redditt   Suffolk variation of Readett, Anglo-Saxon *hreodet* – dweller by the reed bed

Regent   Believed to have come from the Irish name Regane – first recorded in Dublin in 1264 – from the Irish Gaelic name Riagain – little king

Redgrave   Literally means from Redgrave, Suffolk. Redgrave comes from Anglo-Saxon *read graef* meaning reed pit

Rell   Derives from Rolf or Raoul – nickname from the Old Viking for wolf – means son of Raoul

Revans   Nickname for raven – black shiny hair – Several variations but Revans is the Suffolk variation

Riddleston   *Ridel* is Norman French for a small hill – *ton* is Anglo-Saxon for farmland settlement – from a farmland settlement on a small hill from a lost hamlet near or in Polstead

Ridgeon   Suffolk pronunciation of Riching or Richin – Norman French name for son of Rich

Rieman   Suffolk variation of Rayman, Ryman – Anglo-Saxon for dweller by the low lying land or stream

Fredrick Riddleston
(Courtesy of Alan Riddleston)

Ringshall	from Ringshall, which is derived from a nook of land, secluded spot or shelter, *healh* belonging to a Danish chieftain called Hrings Also writ down as Ringshaw
Risby	From Risby Suffolk, and the surname distribution map confirms that. *By* is the Viking equivalent of *burgh*, borough and bury – a fortified hill belonging to Danish chieftain *Hrisa* – Hrisa by
Risher	Suffolk variation of Rusher – from Anglo-Saxon *rysc* meaning rush – dweller among the rushes
Riveron	Norman French – Means from Reveillon, Orne
Rookard	Rookard is Anglo-Saxon for rook yard – someone who lives near a yard with loads a rooks. A yard in medieval times was roughly 30 acres, long and narrow in strips, and was part of the feudal system

May 2 1914

This is my husbands wish
Frederick Riddleston Polstead
if eny thing happen his children
to share every thing alike
Jane Riddleston his wife signed
by Fredick Thomas Riddleston
Arthur Daniel Riddleston
Albert William Riddleston
Amy Riddleston
Harry Riddleston
Frank Riddleston
Herbert Edward Riddleston
George Alfred Riddleston
Jane Riddleston
Witness my husbands signature by Cross
Fredrick Riddleston   +

Last Will and Testament of Fredrick Riddleston, witnessed and signed by all his children and wife. He couldn't read nor write so he signed with a +
(Courtesy of Alan Riddleston)

*George Henry Ridgeon 1896 – 1916,
George served with the 7th Suffolk
Regiment and was killed in action on
the 3rd day of the Battle of the
Somme. Top left, George as a young
boy. Above, Deadman's Penny.
Below Funeral Card.
(Courtesy of Chris Ridgeon)*

Rozier   Number of variations – but Rozier is the Suffolk variation.
It's a Huguenot Protestant refugee surname – a grower of
roses – rose petals were used in the medieval period for
medicines as well as for perfume and textile dyes.

Ruffels   Viking name via the Normans – *hrodwulf* later *hrolfr* –
nickname associated with the wolf – Ruffels was recorded
later in Norman times as a diminutive of Rolf

*Darren Rozier, of BBC Radio Suffolk, dressed as St Edmund,
at the launch of the '**St Edmund for England**' campaign.
Supported by Greene King Brewery and BBC Radio Suffolk
(Courtesy of Darren Rozier, BBC Radio Suffolk)*

Ruman   *Rue* is Anglo-Saxon for dweller in a row of houses. In Suffolk only is the name extended – the man who lives in a row of houses

Rumbellow local nickname for a sailor – from the meaningless combination of syllables sung as a refrain whilst rowing –
**Hal an tow, Jolly rumbelow,
We were up, Long before the day 0**

S

Sarff   Suffolk variation of the Viking word for cormorant – *skarfrs*. Also recorded is Suffolk as **Scarff** and **Scarce**

Saver   Suffolk variation of the surname Saffer from the Norman French *saffre* meaning a glutton

Sawer   From Anglo-Saxon *sawere* – to sow – someone who sows seed.

Scates   Middle English *scate* or *scaite* – the fish. Therefore a nickname for seller of fish. Scates would be the son of the fish seller

Scoggins   Suffolk variation of Viking nickname *Skoggi* – meaning the bearded one. Scoggins means the son of the bearded one

Scotchmer   Refers to another lost village in Suffolk, Scotchmere – so called because there would have been an Irish settlement by a lake – *Scottas* was Anglo-Saxon and Old Viking for Irish

Scowen   Derives from both the Anglo-Saxon and Ancient Celt. Anglo-Saxons adopted it from the Ancient Britons – Dweller near an elderberry plantation or maker of elderberry wine

Scribner   Many variations of this name – From Norman French *escrivain*, writer or copier of books and manuscripts. The 'v' sound hardens up to sound more like 'b'. So from *escrivain* we get *escribain*, from which we get Scribner – and words like scribe and scribble

Seely   Many variations of this name – Sealy, Sealey, Selly, Ceely, Ceeley, Sealig, etc etc – but Seely is the Suffolk variation. Comes from the Anglo-Saxon *sealig* meaning holy and often misused in the phrase 'Silly Suffolk'

Segers   Many variations, and quite a wide distribution – Segers is the Suffolk variation. Anglo-Saxon *sagar* for sea spear – a sea warrior

Selvage   Many variations, but Selvage is Suffolk. Comes from the Norman French *salvage* or *sauvage*, meaning savage and wild

Seman   Many variations, but **Seamans** and **Seman** are Suffolk. First recorded in the Domesday Book 1086 and is Anglo-Saxon for a sea man – sailor

Shafe   Many variations – Shafe is the Suffolk variation. Comes from the Anglo-Saxon *sceagh* – dweller by the wood

Shinn   From the Anglo-Saxon *scinn* – pronounced *shin* by the Anglo-Saxons and *skin* by the Vikings – it's a trade name for a skinner

Sillett   Norman French for son of Sill – and Sill being short for Sylvester

Simper — First recorded, 1674 Suffolk Hearth Tax referring to Geoffrey de Clinton, chamberlain to Henry I, who came from Saint Pierre de Semilly, Normandy. Simper literally means from Saint Pierre

Sissell — Suffolk dialect way of saying Cecil – and only recorded as Sissell in Suffolk – Cecil was the patron saint of *musicians*

Skeet — There are other variations which are East Anglian, but Skeet is Suffolk. Viking *skjotr* for being fast, quick, fleet of foot.

Songer — Anglo-Saxon *songere* for a church singer – a chorister

Spall — Many variations, – Spall is the Suffolk variation. An Old English byname recorded afore the Domesday Book. A dialect way of saying St Paul – someone associated with a church called St Paul

Spindler — Anglo-Saxon for a maker of spindles

Spoore/ Spore — Anglo-Saxon *spura* meaning spur – a spurrier

Spraggins — Son of Spragg – and Spragg means someone who is lively

Squirrell — Norman French – *le esquirel* – later *le squirrel*. A nickname for someone lively and agile

Staff — Anglo-Saxon used by Chaucer as a type of leanness or thinness

Stallworth
Stallworthy
Stollery — All three names derive from the lost 13th Century, Suffolk village of Stallworth or Stallworthy. Stollery is the local dialect pronunciation of that place name.

Stammer — Anglo-Saxon – *stanmer* – meaning 'stone fame' – someone who stands firm

Stanard — Many variations – eg Stanhard, Stanhart, Stannard and Stanart – but Stanard is the Suffolk variation – Anglo-Saxon nickname *Stanheard* – stone hard – a good warrior – or someone who stands by his faith – etc etc – immoveable

Starn — **Starns, Stearne, Stearns.** Many other variations but these are the Suffolk ones – Anglo-Saxon *styrne* meaning severe.

Steff, Stiff — Anglo-Saxon for unyielding and strong, uncompromising, austere

Steggals, Stegal — Many variations but these two are Suffolk – dweller by the style. These are Saxon names from the Anglo-Saxon word *stigol*, Angle pronunciation *Styel* – style – hence the surname 'Styles'

Suggate — Suggate is Suffolk variation – dweller by the south gate

Anna, daughter of Louisa Stollery,
with her daughter Ellen Jane
(Courtesy of Mary Oliver)

Suttle   Distribution maps show two locations – Suffolk and Yorkshire. The Yorkshire Suttle literally means from Soothill, Yorkshire. The Suffolk Suttle means crafty and cunning from the Norman-French word *sotil*

Syrett   Many variations , but Syrett is the Suffolk variation – Anglo-Saxon *sigeraed* – with the Angle pronunciation of syred or syrett meaning victory counsel – a successful warrior and leader

T

Thurkell   Many variations – but Thurkell is Suffolk and a less common variation of Thurkettle – Viking for Thor's Kettle. A Kettle in Norse mythology, is a special cauldron from whence warriors are made – a special warrior from Thor's Kettle

Tigar,
Teager   Norman-French *tigier* or Anglo-Saxon *thiodger* – people's spear – a warrior

Tongate   Someone who lives by the ton gate or the town gate

Tydeman   Suffolk variation of Tiddeeman from Anglo-Saxon *teodingmann*. The chief man of a tithing, originally ten householders

U

Ungless   Quote from Oxford Dictionary of English Surnames, 'The *Suffolk example, Ungle, makes it clear we are concerned with only one name, the Viking, Ulfkettle – meaning wolf cauldron – which is common in that county*'. In Viking mythology many warriors came from the cauldron (kettle) – from the wolf's kettle comes the protective warrior – and Ungless means the son of Ungle

Upston   The 'B' often softens up to a 'P'. Literally, someone from Ubbeston. Sometimes as **Upson**,

V

Vandeville   Derives from a Dutch name meaning *van der veld*. Someone who lives or makes a living 'from the field'

Vineyard   A Suffolk variation of Winyard, Wingard. A worker in the vineyard and comes from the Anglo-Saxon *win geard*

W

Wansey   Norman-French – from Wanchy in Seine-Inferieure

Washbrook   From Washbrook, Suffolk

Watsham   From Wattisham in Suffolk

Went   From the Middle English *wente* – where roads met or crossed Therefore dweller by the road junction

Westbroom
   A lost Suffolk village which is now incorporated in Woolpit

Wetheringsett
   From Wetheringsett in Suffolk

William Baden Whatling and Annie Durrant. Wedding photo circa 1923–4
(Courtesy of Gary Wilson)

Whatling Other variations are more widespread – Whatling is very Suffolk. From the Anglo-Saxon *Hwaetling – Hwaet ling* – son of *Hwaet – hwaet* means active, bold and brave

Whayman Suffolk variation of Wyman. From Anglo-Saxon – *wigmund* – pronounced Whaymand – War Protector

Whistlecraft Anglo-Saxon – dweller at a croft by a *twisla* – a fork in the river

Whymark The Suffolk variation is with the 'h'. They were Breton mercenaries in 1066 and the Breton name was *Wuihomarch* – a warrior worthy to have a horse – a cavalryman

George Whymark. Gardener to
Sir William Brunyate 1935
(Courtesy of Vonny Whymark)

Winney   Anglo-Saxon – *Wyngoefu* – meaning 'Joy Battle' also as Winny

Woolnough Other variations, but Woolnough is the Suffolk one. Anglo-Saxon nickname relating to the legendary wolf. Means 'wolf boldness'

Worledge   Plus many variations, such as **Walladge**, **Wolledge**, **Worlidge** – They are all truly Suffolk. Anglo-Saxon name deriving from the wolf meaning worthy, noble and distinguished.

Lewis Walladge 1878–1945
(Courtesy of Keith Walladge)

Wortham   from Wortham

Whybread from Weybred

Wiskins   Viking pronunciation of Anglo-Saxon *wisc* – dweller near a damp meadow or marsh – Wiskin means – family of Wisk, and Wiskins means son of Wiskin

Woolby   From a lost Suffolk hamlet – Viking for wolf plus fortified hill

Wrycraft   Anglo-Saxon *ryge* – pronounced rye by the Angles plus 'croft' – Means dweller by the rye croft

Y

Yonwin   Anglo-Saxon 'young friend'

CHAPTER 5

Where Have All The Fishing Gone? Long Time Passing

Yes indeed! Where *have* all the fishing gone?

Through the centuries, from Anglo-Saxon times onwards, all along the Suffolk coast, there were many large fishing fleets running out of Lowestoft, Dunwich, Slaughden and Southwold. Other fishing villages would have smaller fishing fleets, and where it was not possible to have a quay or jetty, they moored and off loaded their catch on the beach.

Coastal erosion has seen the disappearance of the fishing fleets at Dunwich and Slaughden, as explained in one of my previous books, 'Caw'd a Hell', under the chapter about the ever changing Suffolk coastline. But there are many other reasons showing the rise and fall of this once very vital industry.

There were two main components to the fishing industry. Firstly, there were the herring luggers, which also caught mackerel. The luggers were so called because the lug sail (pron lugs'll), was shaped like an ear, or lug. Secondly, there were the trawling fleets, for cod, plaice, haddock and skate.

Fishermen on the beach at Southwold
(Courtesy Suffolk Record Office – Ipswich ref – K681/1/414/151)

Herring Market, Lowestoft c. 1900 Peacock & Co
(Courtesy Suffolk Record Office, Lowestoft ref FMK/12a 1300/72/21/15)

During the 1800s there was an upsurge in the demand for fish, and the industry boomed, especially Lowestoft. After the Napoleonic Wars, the country saw a dramatic increase in population, which meant a huge increase in the demand for fish. Although there was mass unemployment and civil unrest, the fishing industry bucked the trend. The building of the railways meant faster inland transport, and as a result, more fish was being carried from the ports to cities and towns to cater for an ever increasing demand, especially from the fast growing industrial towns at the time.

Lowestoft

Lowestoft was not the main fishing port in Suffolk until the mid 1800s, and then she became one of the biggest in the country, let alone in Suffolk.

It all started in Norfolk, with a dispute twixt Norwich and Great Yarmouth, between the Norwich businessmen and the port. There were arguments over payments, transport costs etc. So the Norwich business-men decided to build a Norwich/Lowestoft navigation system, by simply joining the River Yare to Lake Lothing. This was a far happier situation, as the journey would be ten miles shorter, and Lake Lothing, which was one mile long and three hundred yards wide, was to become a safe salt water haven for the fleet. The quay area in Lowestoft was also extensively expanded at the time to suit the needs.

New Herring Market and Fish Wharf c. 1910
(Courtesy Suffolk Record Office, Lowestoft ref FMK/12a 1300/72/21/8)

Lowestoft was booming, not just with the increase in the size of the fleet, but all the associated trades that went with it. Boatyards, shipwrights, ship builders, coopers for fish barrels, chandlers, rope walks, net makers, wherries to carry the ice, curing houses for the kippers, hard smoked red herrings and bloaters....the list is endless. Gaelic speaking Scottish fisher girls would come down by train to gut and pack the herring for the season. The hard smoked red herrings were sent to the Mediterranean in fast sailing brigs and brigantines – packages of bloaters and fresh iced herring went by train to the fast growing industrial towns.

In the 1860s many herring luggers were being fitted out for trawling, when the autumn herring season was over. By 1880 there were: 312 draft fishing boats, 139 trawlers, employing some 815 men and boys, including 'joskins'. The herring season followed the harvest and 'joskins' was the name given to the landlubbers coming from the farms after harvest time, looking for work during the herring season, and whose principal job on board boat was helping to haul in the nets.

By 1913, there were a staggering six hundred fishing vessels sailing out of Lowestoft alone! Today you'd be lucky to count them on two hands! Seven at the last count!

Hard Times, Good Times, Hard Times

It was not all that rosy at sea, and it was a hard life, but paid well. If you had a good catch that is. The term 'half and halfers' was commonly used, and meant that the owner of the boat, usually the skipper, got half the profit from the sale of their catch, and the crew shared the other half.

It was a very dangerous job, and many lives were lost. The storms and gales in January 1895 in particular took its deadly toll, and saw a multitude of casualties. Not just from Lowestoft, not just from Suffolk, but from the whole of the East Coast. A similar event happened again on a notorious day in October 1889, where literally hundreds and hundreds of lives were lost to a watery grave. Suffolk fishermen did not escape this disaster, and they had their share of the staggering numbers that perished.

A very famous folk song marks the event, and although not specifically Suffolk, it includes the whole of the East Coast. I can assure you, when this song is sung in a Suffolk folk club, or at a folk session (and it's sung very regularly), everyone will join in. It is community singing at its absolute best, especially at the Everyman's Folk Club in Stratford St Andrew. It is sung passionately, but with due reverence, and very moving – a lump comes to my throat every time I hear it being sung.

Three Score and Ten

Methinks I see a host of craft
Spreading their sails alee,
As down the Humber they do glide
All bound for the northern sea.
Methinks I see on each small craft
A crew with hearts so brave,
Setting out to earn their daily bread,
Upon the restless wave.

And it's three-score-and-ten, Boys and men,
Were lost from Grimsby Town,
From Yarmouth down to Scarborough,
Many hundreds more were drowned.
Our herring craft, our trawlers,
Our fishing smacks as well,
They long to fight that bitter night,
And battle with the swell.

Methinks I see 'em yet again
As they leave the land behind,
Casting their nets into the sea,
Those fishing shoals to find.
Methinks I see 'em yet again
And all on board's all right,
With sails close-reefed and decks cleared up
And sidelights burning bright.

And it's three-score-and-ten, Boys and men,
Were lost from Grimsby Town,
From Yarmouth down to Scarborough,
Many hundreds more were drowned.
Our herring craft, our trawlers,
Our fishing smacks as well,
They long to fight that bitter night,
And battle with the swell.

October's night was such a sight,
'twas never seen before,
When masts and spars and broken yards
Came floating to the shore.
There was many a heart of sorrow,
There was many a heart so brave,
There was many a hearty fisher lad
Who found a watery grave.

And it's three-score-and-ten, Boys and men,
Were lost from Grimsby Town,
From Yarmouth down to Scarborough,
Many hundreds more were drowned.
Our herring craft, our trawlers,
Our fishing smacks as well,
They long to fight that bitter night,
And battle with the swell.

The 1914-18 War saw many losses too. Especially the Q-boats. These were Anti U-boat craft under disguise and – in fact – some were converted fishing boats armed only with a three pounder gun. One famous incident led to Tom Crisp DSC, the skipper of the Q-boat 'Nelson' (who had been very successful in detecting U-boats), taking on the enemy. He was mortally wounded, having both his legs shot away. But he did not 'lower the flag' and saved all the men, including his son who was a member of the crew. Before his last brave act he was able to send a message for help attached to 'Red Cock', a carrier pigeon. Tom knew he was at an end, so he ordered his son, also Tom, 'Throw me over boy … throw the confidential book over too … I am done for'. This last act of bravery ensured the crew concentrated on escaping from both the enemy and the sinking fishing vessel, and into the row boat. A Navy ship in dock received the message for help and retrieved the lifeboat with all the crew on board, except Tom Crisp Snr, who was later posthumously awarded the Victoria Cross.

Up to the 1920s the railways were used to get fish to market. But thereafter, the rise in road transport meant even more markets were opening up for the fish industry, and the Suffolk fishing industry was booming up to the 1950s.

Tom Crisp with his DSC medal (Courtesy of Tom Crisp's Relatives and Suffolk Record Office, Lowestoft, ref – Biographies Tom Crisp VC)

The Decline

Howsumever, during the 1950s and 60s the shoals of herring started to dwindle, as did other fish, principally the cod. Had it been overfished? I don't think so.

Although there were international agreements on fishing boundaries, not all the nations agreed with them. So into our waters they came, with smaller gauge nets. This had the effect of not only taking out this season's adult fish, but also the smaller young fish as well (next season's mums and dads). . . they were breaking the reproduction cycle. The English nets were bigger, and let the younger ones through, allowing the fish to constantly reproduce … Sensible!

Then came the 'Cod Wars' with Iceland in the early 1970s, with even more fishing boundary disputes. However, the British government backed down and *done* a U-turn, (nothing new). Because Iceland was such a small place, Britain did not want to emerge as a 'bully boy' in the arena of international politics and diplomacy.

During this time we also joined the Common Market, which was a European free trade association, which Britain voted to stay in. Ted Heath, the Prime Minister, had signed us up without a referendum, and Harold Wilson, the next PM, went to the nation, and we voted to stay in a free trade association (wish we had listened to De Gaulle's, 'Non! Non! Non!'). This common market was eventually to become known as the EU, the European Union, and a far cry from its original intentions to be a simple trading partnership.

The net result for our fishermen, was the introduction of the Common Fisheries Policy. This meant that other nations could now fish our waters with smaller nets. At the same time, our own fishermen were given quotas, reducing the number of catches. They were not allowed to exceed that quota. This action made way for foreign fleets to plunder our waters. Not only that, the ludicrous quota system applied to each catch brought home, and not based on a time scale. So if a fisherman was two ton over weight, he had to throw two ton of dead fish back into the sea, (seagulls saying, "thank you very much"), and was not able to offset it against the next trip. If caught bringing these 'black fish' ashore to market, then there were heavy penalties.

There was a vast reduction in fish stocks. So the EU reduced the quotas even more. This led to 'part-time' fishermen in Suffolk, the industry uneconomical, and many leaving or going bankrupt. The Suffolk ports were affected big time, with a sharp decline in the fishing fleets, and all the associated industries dependent on it.

What we have left today, is a handful of boats running out of Lowestoft, with a number of tiny craft going out to sea from other coastal villages and towns. They land on the beaches, and carry their catch to the black shods dotted along the Suffolk coast. This is largely for local trade who buy freshly caught fish, take it home, and have a scrummy meal that evening. Howsumever, as nice and idyllic as this sounds, it is no consolation for the demise and decimation of the Suffolk fishing industry, and the hardship it has brought!

Black shods on the beach
Drawing of Low Light and Beach, Lowestoft, 1851
(Courtesy Suffolk Record Office, Lowestoft ref FMK/12a 1300/72/2/3)

DON'T HURRY ME – I'M SUFFOLK

(Courtesy of Mary Oliver)

The End